Throughout Susan Seddon Boulet's paintings runs a strong current of mythology and folklore. The artist has delved deep into the essence of myths and folktales from many lands. She explores the mystery and meaning of inner and outer mythologies—the ones we create within ourselves and the ones embedded in our cross-cultural traditions. Many of her paintings focus on stories and myths involving real and imaginary animals and the relationship between those animals and humans. Pomegranate is proud to feature thirty of these enchanting pieces in this bestiary.

To appreciate these paintings, of course, it is not necessary to have a deep and abiding interest in mythology and folklore. The images, powerful yet playful, alive with refreshing imagination, can be to us whatever we make of them. As with all of her work, this group of paintings reaches out to the viewer, irresistibly enveloping all within its magical and calm embrace.

Born in Brazil of British parents, Susan Seddon Boulet was raised in South America and educated there and in Switzerland. Now a resident of the San Francisco Bay Area, she has received many awards in northern California art exhibitions. Her work can be found in private collections throughout the United States as well as in South America, Europe and Asia.

All of Susan Seddon Boulet's originals reproduced in this book of postcards were created using oil pastel, ink and pencil on artboard.

A Susan Seddon Boulet Bestiary

A Book of Postcards

Pomegranate Artbooks, San Francisco

Pomegranate Artbooks
Box 808022
Petaluma, CA 94975

ISBN 0-87654-812-5
Pomegranate Catalog No. A581

Pomegranate publishes several other postcard collections on many different subjects.
Please write to the publisher for more information.

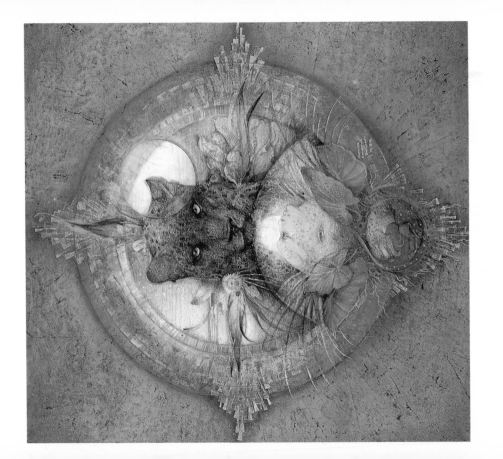

A Susan Seddon Boulet Bestiary

The JAGUAR is a Mexican messenger of the Forest Spirits. In Peruvian shamanic tradition, it is associated with the direction west, where one must meet it, die and be reborn as the Rainbow Jaguar.

Pomegranate • Box 808022 • Petaluma, CA 94975

Susan
Seddon
Boulet
1988

A Susan Seddon Boulet Bestiary

The WOLF was an important figure for many North American native peoples. It was often seen as the coyote's brother and counterpart to the raven or as the ruler of the country of the dead. In Norse mythology, the wolf could swallow the sun and the moon. Here it is depicted as a guide to other realms.

Pomegranate • Box 808022 • Petaluma, CA 94975

Susan Seddon Boulet
1987

A Susan Seddon Boulet Bestiary

The RAVEN was the hero/trickster of the North Pacific Coast tribes. It drew humankind from the clam shell, stole fire and the sun, brought into being water and animals, created and recreated all of nature. It was depicted as being sometimes clever and sometimes foolhardy, either in animal or in human form.

Pomegranate • Box 808022 • Petaluma, CA 94975

Susan Ecklund Bratlet
AUG-1987

A Susan Seddon Boulet Bestiary

In folklore and legend, the COYOTE, the creator, trickster and culture hero, almost always belongs to the mythical age when animals talked, behaved and lived like human beings. As culture hero, one of its acts was to secure light, fire or the sun. Its more earthy side was forever getting it into trouble.

Pomegranate • Box 808022 • Petaluma, CA 94975

A Susan Seddon Boulet Bestiary

The MERMAID was a supernatural being, half maiden and half fish, associated with the goddess Marian and connected by the Greeks to Aphrodite. Mermaids were known at times to rescue drowning mariners and at others to lure them to their doom. Their greatest wish was for a human soul.

Pomegranate • Box 808022 • Petaluma, CA 94975

A Susan Seddon Boulet Bestiary

The GRYPHON was a fabulous beast. Part eagle and part
lion, it was the guardian of treasures. It shares the
symbolism of the dragon in the East. It was connected to
the sun, especially at dawn, when the light turns to gold.

Pomegranate • Box 808022 • Petaluma, CA 94975

A Susan Seddon Boulet Bestiary

The Greek SPHINX had the head and breasts of a woman, the body and feet of a lion, and the wings of an eagle. She was the guardian of the enigma. Anyone unable to answer her riddle was punished by death. She symbolized the mysterious and embodied the four elements.

Pomegranate • Box 808022 • Petaluma, CA 94975

A Susan Seddon Boulet Bestiary

The HALCYON was named for Alcyone, daughter of Aeolus, god of the wind. Grieving for her drowned husband, Alcyone attempted to drown herself as well. But before entering the water she transformed into a bird. The gods pitied her and changed her husband into a living bird also.

Pomegranate • Box 808022 • Petaluma, CA 94975

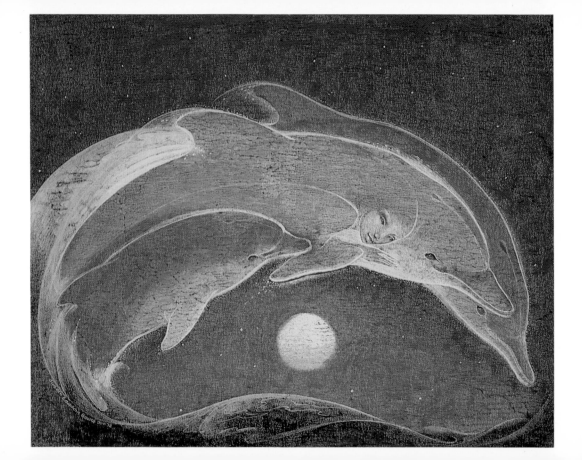

A Susan Seddon Boulet Bestiary

The DOLPHIN's role as friend of humankind is found in many ancient legends. In Greek myth, the gods rewarded the dolphin for its helpfulness by placing it in the heavens as one of their constellations.

Pomegranate • Box 808022 • Petaluma, CA 94975

A Susan Seddon Boulet Bestiary

The Greeks believed the moon created the CAT. Ancient tradition associated the widening and narrowing of the cat's eyes with the waxing and waning of the moon.

Pomegranate • Box 808022 • Petaluma, CA 94975

A Susan Seddon Boulet Bestiary

In the beginning, the HARPIES were winged goddesses who carried weapons of gold. Later they became divinities resembling vultures, but with women's faces. They were swifter than birds and winds and associated with storms. They had a hunger that could not be satisfied and would swoop down from the mountains and snatch away food laid out for feasts.

Pomegranate • Box 808022 • Petaluma, CA 94975

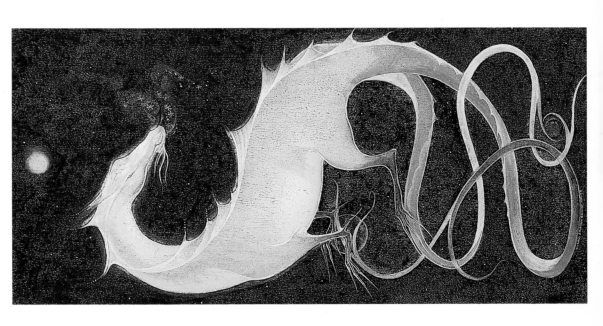

A Susan Seddon Boulet Bestiary

Taking new forms according to its surroundings yet never taking final shape, the DRAGON symbolized change and was associated with the forces of nature. Perhaps the most famous of all the ancient mythical beasts, it was the hoarder of great treasures.

Pomegranate • Box 808022 • Petaluma, CA 94975

A Susan Seddon Boulet Bestiary

The BEAR was sacred to the Finno-Ugric people. In alchemy it was related to the instincts and to all initial stages. It was regarded as a lunar animal and was associated with Diana. The bear was deeply respected in North American myth as a source of great strength, power and healing.

Pomegranate • Box 808022 • Petaluma, CA 94975

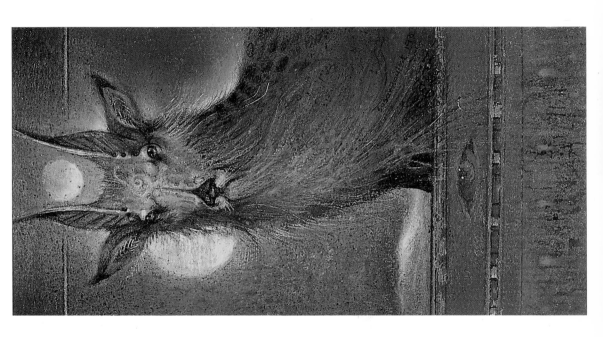

A Susan Seddon Boulet Bestiary

On the full moon, the MOONBEAST had the power to grant one's fondest wish. But if the wish brought harm to another, the wisher was banished forever to the dark side of the moon.

Pomegranate • Box 808022 • Petaluma, CA 94975

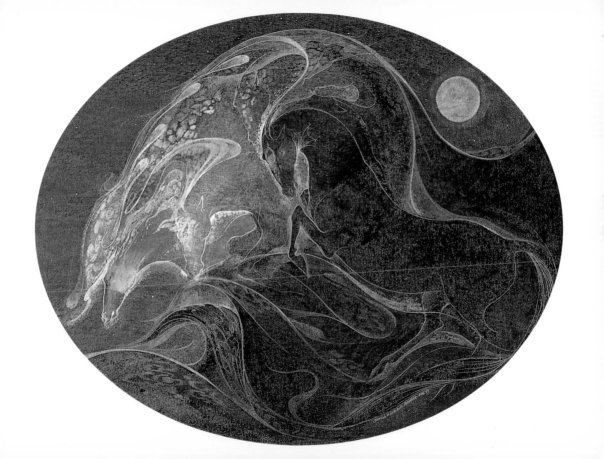

A Susan Seddon Boulet Bestiary

"The SEA HORSE is like the horse of dry land, but its mane and its tail grow longer; its colour is more lustrous and its hooves are cleft like those of wild oxen, while its height is no less than the land horse's and slightly larger than the ass's." —*Zakariyya al-Qaswini,*
thirteenth-century cosmographer

Pomegranate • Box 808022 • Petaluma, CA 94975

A Susan Seddon Boulet Bestiary

Suchos, the CROCODILE, was the Egyptian god of water.
His sweat became the Nile, and he made the "herbage
green." He was connected to Osiris, Egyptian god of
agriculture, who ruled over life, crops, vegetation and
growth, and the Nile and its flood cycle.

Pomegranate • Box 808022 • Petaluma, CA 94975

A Susan Seddon Boulet Bestiary

THE COUNCIL OF IMAGINARY BEASTS was created when the world was new—in the mythic time when humans and animals spoke the same language—to be the keepers of the mysteries in the realm of our imaginings.

Pomegranate • Box 808022 • Petaluma, CA 94975

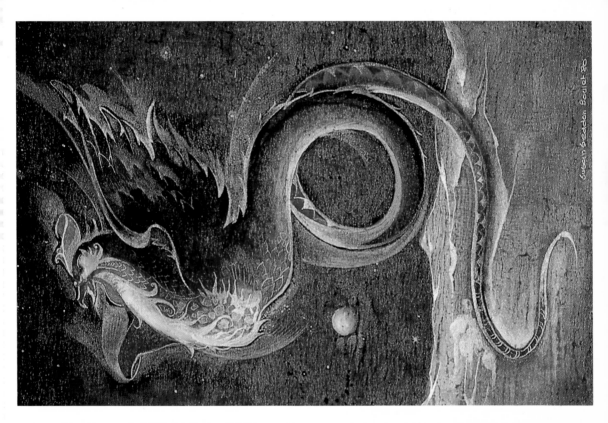

A Susan Seddon Boulet Bestiary

The COCKATRICE was capable of killing a person with a single glance from its glowing eyes. A winged beast with the body of a cock or wyvern (dragon) and always the tail of a wyvern, it was so poisonous that its habitat became the first desert.

Pomegranate • Box 808022 • Petaluma, CA 94975

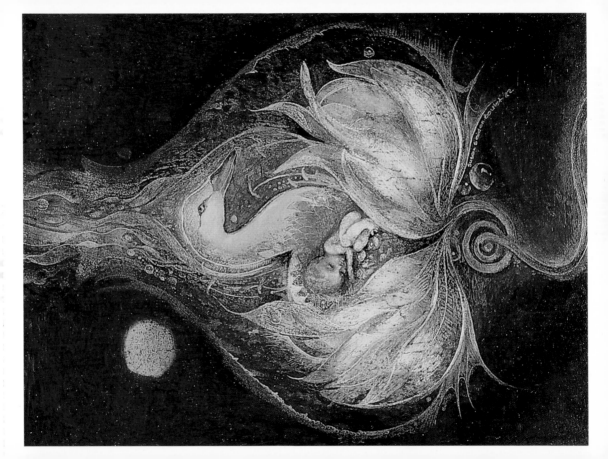

A Susan Seddon Boulet Bestiary

The GOOSE, a solar bird, was important in Finno-Ugric, Siberian-Ostyak, Egyptian and Greek mythologies. It was associated with the Hindu god Brahma. The cosmic gander ridden by Brahma represented his creative principal and symbolized freedom attained through spiritual purity.

Pomegranate • Box 808022 • Petaluma, CA 94975

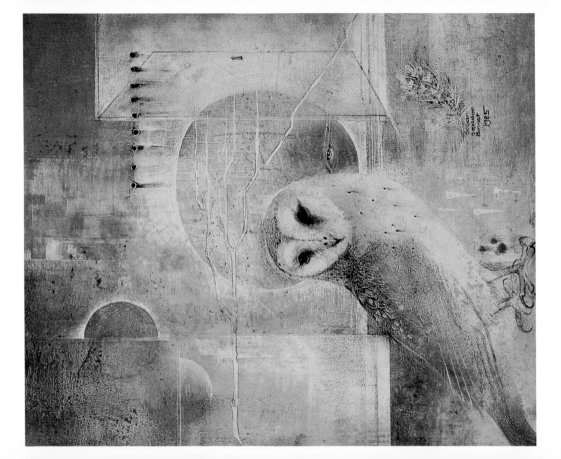

A Susan Seddon Boulet Bestiary

To the Pima Indians, the OWL symbolized the souls of the
dead. An owl hooting at the time of death was believed to
be waiting for the soul of the dying person. To help him or
her into the next world, a dying person was always given
owl feathers.

Pomegranate • Box 808022 • Petaluma, CA 94975

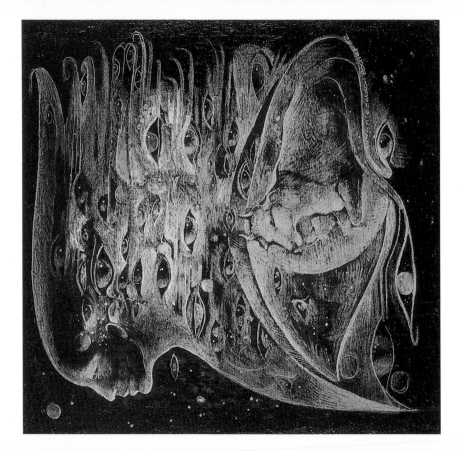

A Susan Seddon Boulet Bestiary

IO was turned into a beautiful white heifer by Zeus to protect her from Hera's wrath. But crafty Hera asked Zeus to give her the heifer as a gift and then put Io in the watchful care of Argus, who had 100 eyes.

Pomegranate • Box 808022 • Petaluma, CA 94975

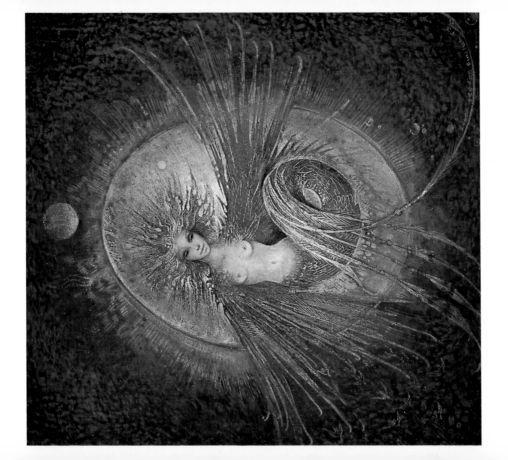

A Susan Seddon Boulet Bestiary

The YOUWARKEE belonged to a race of flying people from a lost island in the Antarctic seas. Half angel and half bird, her body covered with silky down, she had the ability to open her arms and turn them into wings.

Pomegranate • Box 808022 • Petaluma, CA 94975

A Susan Seddon Boulet Bestiary

The PHOENIX was said to have risen from its own ashes and was symbolic of rebirth and regeneration. It represents the sun, which sets as a ball of fire each evening and rises again the following morning.

Pomegranate • Box 808022 • Petaluma, CA 94975

Susan Seddon Boulet may '80

A Susan Seddon Boulet Bestiary

The ROCKINGHORSEFLY, as described in Lewis Carroll's
Through the Looking Glass, is made up entirely of wood and
gets about by swinging from branch to branch. It lives on
sap and sawdust.

Pomegranate • Box 808022 • Petaluma, CA 94975

A Susan Seddon Boulet Bestiary

One widely held ancient belief was that there were only
female TIGERS. The father of all tigers was the West Wind.

Pomegranate • Box 808022 • Petaluma, CA 94975

A Susan Seddon Boulet Bestiary

The fleet and wary UNICORN was often persecuted by humankind for the magical and medicinal properties of its horn. Not only was it a powerful aphrodisiac, but when dipped in water it would repel venomous creatures. The unicorn was associated with the feminine lunar principles and with purity and chastity.

Pomegranate • Box 808022 • Petaluma, CA 94975

A Susan Seddon Boulet Bestiary

The CAPRICORN GOAT has a fish's tail, symbolizing our dual tendency toward the depths (water) and the heights (the mountains) and our passage to or away from the wheel of rebirth. The child is symbolic of new life.

Pomegranate • Box 808022 • Petaluma, CA 94975

A Susan Seddon Boulet Bestiary

CERNUNNOS, "the horned one," was a Celtic or pre-Celtic
god associated with fertility, wealth and the underworld.

Pomegranate • Box 808022 • Petaluma, CA 94975

A Susan Seddon Boulet Bestiary

In Greek mythology, PEGASUS was a divine winged horse that sprang from the blood of the slain Medusa. It was caught and tamed by Athena and presented to the Muses. It became the steed of heroes and poets.

Pomegranate • Box 808022 • Petaluma, CA 94975

A Susan Seddon Boulet Bestiary

The FOX is a magical animal of Japanese folklore, a shape-shifter who bewitches people and assumes human form—sometimes monk, sometimes maiden.

Pomegranate • Box 808022 • Petaluma, CA 94975